For Such a Time Esther's Courageous Stand

Joshua Rhoades

Published by Joshua Paul Rhoades, 2024.

FOR SUCH A TIME ESTHER'S COURAGEOUS STAND

First edition. September 30, 2024.

ISBN: 979-8227867865

Written by Joshua Rhoades.

Also by Joshua Rhoades

Courage Under Fire: David's Stand On The Battlefield
Jonah's Journey: Voices Of Redemption And Lessons In Obedience
The Furnace Of Faith: 12 Principles From The Heat Of Faith
Whispers of Hope: Inspiring Stories of Men's Prayers In Scripture
Frontier Legends: The Oregon Dream
Elijah: A Beacon Of Boldness
HOOK, LINE & SAVIOUR - Faith Reflections from Fishing
Driven By Faith: Motor Racing Inspired Christian Life
30 Day Devotional - Bold and Strong- Coffee Devotions for a Courageous
Christian Walk
Authentic Christianity: The Heart of Old Time Religion
Consider The Ant - God's Tiny Preachers
Flee Fornication: The Plea For Purity
Renewed Hope- How to Find Encouragement in God
Sounding The Call - The Voice of Conviction
The Altar - Where Heaven Meets Earth
The Bible's Battlefields- Timeless Lessons from Ancient Wars
The Sacred Art of Silence - How Silence Speaks in Scripture
Under Fire- The Sanctity of the Traditional Biblical Home
Who Is on the Lord's Side? A Call to Righteousness
What Is Truth? - From Skepticism to Submission
First and Goal- Faith and Football Fundamentals
From Dugout to Devotion- Spiritual Lessons from Baseball
Par for the Course- Faith and Fairways
The Believer's Pace- Tools for Running Life's Marathon
The Immutable Fortress- Security in God's Unchanging Nature
Biblical Bravery
Deer Stands and Devotions: A Hunter's Walk with God

Dedication

To you, the reader, I dedicate "For Such a Time: Esther's Courageous Stand" with the hope and prayer that you will find in these pages the inspiration, courage, and faith to stand strong in your own life, no matter what challenges you face. In a world where fear, uncertainty, and injustice seem to grow with each passing day, Esther's story is as relevant now as it was thousands of years ago. Her journey of bravery, her willingness to risk it all for the sake of truth, and her unwavering trust in God's plan are lessons we can all carry with us.

You, too, are here for a purpose, "for such a time as this." No matter where you find yourself—whether you are in a place of comfort or a season of trial—know that God has placed you exactly where you need to be. The decisions you make, the courage you summon, and the faith you show will not only impact your life but the lives of those around you, just as Esther's did. Perhaps you feel small or unimportant in the grand scheme of things, but remember, Esther was once just an ordinary young woman who found herself in an extraordinary situation. It wasn't her position as queen that gave her strength—it was her faith in God.

As you read through her story, I pray that the lessons from Esther's life will take root in your heart. May you be reminded that courage doesn't mean the absence of fear, but the decision to act despite it. May you learn to trust in God's timing, even when the path ahead seems unclear. And may you be inspired to stand up for what is right, no matter the cost, because God's plans are greater than any fear or doubt that may try to hold you back.

We live in a world that desperately needs people like Esther—people willing to stand for truth and justice. We face moments every day that call us to make hard choices, to be brave, to step out in faith even when we cannot see the outcome. The world around us is filled with challenges, but it is also filled with opportunities for God to work through us. Just as He worked through Esther, He can work through you.

As you turn the pages of this book, remember that you, too, are part of God's story. He has a purpose for you, and no matter what challenges lie ahead, He will give you the strength to face them. You were made for this moment, "for such a time as this." May you rise in courage, walk in faith, and know that through every step you take, God is with you. I dedicate this book to you with a heart full of hope that you will find your own place in God's plan, and that, like Esther, you will stand boldly, bringing honor and glory to His name. Now is the time.

Introduction

In a world filled with uncertainty, fear, and challenges, the story of Esther stands as a powerful reminder of how one person's courage and faith can change the course of history. "For Such a Time: Esther's Courageous Stand" takes us back to a time when Esther, a young Jewish woman, faced an impossible choice. She could remain silent and protect herself, or risk everything—her life, her position, her future—to stand up for what was right and save her people. Esther's story is not just about ancient times; it speaks to us today, in a world where injustice, fear, and difficult decisions seem ever-present. The lessons from her life—courage in the face of fear, faith in the midst of uncertainty, and trusting God's plan even when we cannot see it—are more relevant now than ever. As we walk through her journey, we see that God places each of us in specific circumstances for a reason. Just as Esther was called to act at a critical moment, so too are we called to stand boldly for truth, justice, and love in our own lives. The courage Esther showed, rooted in her faith, is something we are all capable of, through God's strength. As you read, I pray you will find not only inspiration but also the deep conviction that God is calling each of us, for such a time as this, to stand in faith, act with courage, and bring honor and glory to His name, just as Esther did. Now is the time to trust God's plan, step out in faith, and make a difference in the world around us, for His glory.

Chapter 1 - Moment of Crisis

In the biblical story of Esther, one of the most compelling moments is the Moment of Crisis in Esther 4:1, when Mordecai perceives the full impact of the decree made by Haman, which threatens the extermination of the Jewish people in the Persian Empire. In this critical moment, we see Mordecai's deep anguish as he tears his clothes, puts on sackcloth, and mourns openly in the streets of the city. His actions highlight the gravity of the situation and signify a desperate need for divine intervention. Mordecai's response isn't merely an emotional outburst; it's a deliberate and public cry for help. He knows that without intervention, his people face annihilation. His mourning captures the attention of the Jewish community, and it also brings the crisis to the forefront of Esther's awareness. This moment of deep grief serves as a turning point, where the quiet and seemingly distant problem becomes personal for Esther. Although Esther is living in the royal palace, far removed from the immediate threat, this is the moment when Mordecai sets the stage for her to make a courageous choice that will change everything.

The lesson here is powerful: in moments of crisis, we are often faced with decisions that require courage and action, even when the outcome is uncertain. Mordecai's grief is not passive; it is a call to action, a plea for Esther to understand the severity of the situation and to step into her role as a deliverer for her people. The crisis forces Esther to confront her identity—not just as the queen of Persia, but as a Jewish woman who has been placed in this royal position for a greater purpose. Mordecai's sorrow, his sackcloth, and his public mourning serve as reminders that in times of great distress, we cannot remain silent or inactive. The moment of crisis in the story of Esther teaches us that when everything seems to be falling apart, we must look for opportunities to be courageous, to take action, and to trust that we are where we are for a reason.

Esther's initial reaction to Mordecai's mourning is one of concern, but also hesitation. She sends him clothes to replace his sackcloth, as if to offer comfort without fully understanding the depth of the crisis. It is a natural response to want to ease someone's pain without fully engaging in the situation. But Mordecai's refusal to accept the clothes is significant—it is his way of saying that this crisis cannot be avoided or dismissed. He sends a message back to Esther, explaining the decree of death against their people and urging her to go before the king to plead for their lives. This is where the story takes a sharp turn, as Esther is faced with a choice: will she remain silent and hope for the best, or will she risk everything to save her people?

Esther's position as queen gives her a unique opportunity to intervene, but it also comes with great risk. In Persian law, no one could approach the king without being summoned, under penalty of death. Esther's initial hesitation is understandable—approaching the king uninvited could mean losing her life. But Mordecai's response to her hesitation is both direct and profound: "Who knoweth whether thou art come to the kingdom for such a time as this?" (Esther 4:14). Mordecai's words cut to the heart of the matter. He reminds Esther that her rise to the position of queen was not accidental, but part of a divine plan. She has been placed in this position of influence for a reason, and this moment of crisis is her opportunity to fulfill her purpose.

The lesson we learn from this moment is that we all face times when we are called to make difficult, courageous choices. Esther's story reminds us that sometimes we are placed in certain situations, not for our own comfort or advancement, but to serve a greater purpose. The crisis in Esther's life forced her to confront the reality that her royal position came with responsibility—not just to herself, but to her people. In the same way, we are often placed in situations where we have the ability to make a difference, and it is in those moments that we must choose whether to act or to remain silent.

Esther's choice to act is a moment of profound courage. After days of fasting and seeking God's guidance, she resolves to go before the king, saying, "If I perish, I perish" (Esther 4:16). This statement is not one of despair, but of determination. Esther understands the risk, but she is willing to lay down her life for the sake of her people. This is the essence of courage—not the absence of fear, but the willingness to act in spite of it. Esther's bravery is not reckless; it is rooted in her faith in God's sovereignty and her understanding that she has been placed in this position for a reason.

The crisis in Esther's story leads her to make a choice that would not only save her people, but also define her legacy. Her willingness to stand up for what was right, even at great personal risk, is a powerful example for us today. We live in a world where crises are all around us—whether they are personal, societal, or global—and we are often faced with choices that require courage. The story of Esther challenges us to consider how we respond in moments of crisis. Do we shrink back in fear, or do we step forward in faith, trusting that we have been placed in our circumstances for a purpose?

Esther's courageous choice also teaches us about the importance of using our influence for good. As queen, Esther had access to the king in a way that no one else did. She could have chosen to remain silent, to protect her own safety, and to distance herself from the plight of her people. But instead, she used her position of influence to advocate for justice and to save lives. In the same way, we are often given opportunities to use our influence—whether in our families, our communities, or our workplaces—to make a difference. The lesson here is that we should not take our positions of influence lightly. Whether we are in positions of great power or simply have the ear of a friend in need, we are called to use our influence to stand up for what is right, to speak out against injustice, and to point others to God's truth.

The story of Esther's courageous choice is also a reminder of the power of faith in the face of uncertainty. Esther did not know what the outcome of her actions would be. She didn't have any guarantees that the king would extend his scepter to her, or that her plea for her people would be heard. But she acted in faith, trusting that God had placed her in this position for a reason, and that He would guide her steps. In moments of crisis, we too are often faced with uncertainty. We may not know what the outcome of our actions will be, and we may be tempted to give in to fear or doubt. But Esther's story encourages us to step out in faith, trusting that God is in control and that He has a purpose for us in the midst of our crisis.

In conclusion, Esther's Moment of Crisis is a powerful reminder of the importance of courage, faith, and the willingness to act in the face of danger. Her story challenges us to consider how we respond when we are faced with difficult choices. Do we shrink back in fear, or do we step forward in faith, trusting that we have been placed in our circumstances for a purpose? Esther's example teaches us that true courage is not the absence of fear, but the willingness to act in spite of it. It reminds us that we are often given opportunities to use our influence for good, and that we should not take those opportunities lightly. Above all, Esther's story points us to the truth that God is sovereign, and that even in the midst of crisis, He is at work, guiding our steps and using us to fulfill His greater plan. Like Esther, we are called to be courageous in the face of crisis, to trust in God's purpose for our lives, and to use our influence to make a difference in the world around us.

Chapter 2 - Mordecai's Appeal

In the story of Esther, one of the key moments that defines her as a courageous leader is when her cousin Mordecai makes a direct and urgent appeal for her to intervene on behalf of their people. This appeal comes in Esther 4:8, where Mordecai gives a copy of the written decree ordering the destruction of the Jews and asks Esther to take action by going before King Xerxes to plead for their lives. Mordecai's appeal to Esther highlights the urgency of the situation and the necessity for her to step out of her comfort zone, risking her life to save others. Up until this point, Esther has been living relatively safely within the royal palace, shielded from the immediate threat facing her people. But Mordecai's message is clear: the time for silence is over. She cannot remain passive or detached, and her position as queen now requires her to take a stand. This appeal represents a crucial turning point in the story, as it forces Esther to confront the reality of her identity, her responsibility, and her purpose. She may have been chosen as queen through seemingly random circumstances, but Mordecai makes it clear that her rise to this position is not by accident. She has been placed in this role for a reason, and that reason is now staring her in the face. The fate of her people rests on her decision to act.

The lesson from this part of Esther's story is powerful and timeless. Mordecai's appeal to Esther mirrors the moments in our own lives when we are called to step up in difficult circumstances. Just like Esther, we may find ourselves in positions of influence or privilege, and we may be tempted to believe that we can stay silent or uninvolved when crises arise. But Mordecai's words to Esther remind us that there are times when we must use our voice, our platform, and our influence to make a difference. The urgency in Mordecai's appeal highlights the importance of action in the face of injustice. He doesn't sugarcoat the situation for Esther; he makes it clear that the decree is real, the danger is imminent, and the consequences of inaction will be catastrophic. Similarly, there are times in our lives when we are faced with decisions that will have real and lasting consequences for ourselves and others. The world around us may be filled with suffering, injustice, and crisis, and we may be in a unique position to bring about change. But like Esther, we may hesitate, unsure of the risks or fearful of the potential fallout. Mordecai's appeal to Esther is a reminder that sometimes the greatest danger lies not in taking action, but in failing to act.

Mordecai's appeal also underscores the theme of responsibility. Though Esther had lived in the palace, somewhat removed from the immediate concerns of her people, Mordecai's words draw her back to her roots and to the reality of her identity. He reminds her that even though she is queen, she is still a Jew, and her fate is tied to the fate of her people. This moment forces Esther to reckon with the fact that her royal status does not exempt her from responsibility. In fact, her position as queen makes her the only one with the access and influence necessary to make a difference. Mordecai challenges Esther to recognize that her life is not just about her own survival or comfort; she has been placed in her position for a greater purpose. This is a critical lesson for all of us, as it speaks to the idea that we are often placed in certain roles, jobs, or relationships not merely for our own benefit, but to serve others and to fulfill a higher calling. Mordecai's appeal pushes Esther to see that her life has been leading up to this moment, and she has a choice to make—either she can shrink back in fear, or she can embrace her responsibility and act with courage.

When we look at Mordecai's appeal to Esther, we also see a reflection of the importance of standing up for what is right, even when it comes at great personal risk. For Esther, going before the king without being summoned could very well mean death. The laws of the Persian court were strict, and no one, not even the queen, could approach the king without being called. Esther is fully aware of the risk she faces, which is why she initially hesitates. She knows that this is not just a matter of asking for a favor—her very life is on the line. But Mordecai's appeal cuts through the fear and uncertainty. He reminds her that this is a moment where silence is not an option. He tells her that if she remains silent, deliverance for the Jews will come from another place, but she and her family will perish. Mordecai's faith is clear—he believes that God will ultimately save His people, but he also knows that Esther has been placed in a unique position to be part of that salvation. His words challenge Esther, and by extension all of us, to act with faith and courage, even when the personal stakes are high.

Esther's decision to heed Mordecai's appeal is one of the most courageous choices in the Bible. After taking time to fast and pray, she resolves to go before the king, saying, "If I perish, I perish" (Esther 4:16). This statement is a powerful declaration of courage and faith. Esther understands the risks, but she is willing to face them because she knows that this is her moment to act. Her willingness to put her life on the line for the sake of her people is a testament to her strength and selflessness. In this moment, Esther transforms from a young woman who was initially hesitant and unsure into a leader who is willing to face the unknown with bravery. The courage that Esther displays in this moment is a model for all of us, especially when we face situations that require us to stand up for others or take a risk for what is right. It is a reminder that true courage is not the absence of fear, but the decision to act in spite of it.

The story of Esther's courageous choice in response to Mordecai's appeal has deep relevance for us today. In our own lives, we are often confronted with situations where we have the opportunity to make a difference, but it requires us to step out of our comfort zones and take risks. Whether it's standing up against injustice, advocating for someone who cannot speak for themselves, or making a bold decision that could change the course of our lives, we are all faced with moments where we must decide whether we will act with courage or remain silent. Like Esther, we may be tempted to hesitate, to weigh the risks, and to consider the potential consequences. But Mordecai's words remind us that there are times when the cost of inaction is far greater than the risk of action.

Furthermore, Mordecai's appeal to Esther also teaches us about the importance of faith. Throughout the story, we see that Mordecai believes that God is ultimately in control. Even as he urges Esther to act, he expresses confidence that deliverance will come for the Jewish people, even if Esther chooses not to act. This faith in God's sovereignty is a key theme in the story of Esther. While God is not explicitly mentioned in the book, His presence is felt throughout, as events unfold in a way that reveals His hand at work behind the scenes. Mordecai's appeal to Esther is a reminder that while we may be called to take action, we can also trust that God is working through us and around us to accomplish His purposes. This lesson encourages us to step out in faith, knowing that even when we cannot see the whole picture, God is guiding our steps.

In conclusion, Mordecai's appeal to Esther in Esther 4:8 is a pivotal moment in the story, and it carries powerful lessons for us today. His urgent plea for

Esther to intervene reminds us of the importance of taking action in the face of crisis, using our influence for good, and recognizing the responsibility that comes with our positions in life. Esther's response to Mordecai's appeal is a demonstration of incredible courage, as she chooses to risk her life to save her people. Her story challenges us to consider how we will respond when we are called to make difficult, courageous choices. Will we remain silent and hope that someone else will step in, or will we, like Esther, rise to the occasion and act with faith and courage? Mordecai's appeal also teaches us about the importance of faith in God's plan. Even as we take action, we can trust that God is at work, guiding our steps and using us for His purposes. The story of Esther's courageous choice continues to inspire and challenge us to live with boldness, faith, and a commitment to doing what is right, no matter the cost. Just as Esther was called for such a time as this, we too are called to step into the moments where we can make a difference and trust that God is with us every step of the way.

Chapter 3 - Motivation through Fear

In the story of Esther, one of the most striking themes is her Motivation through Fear, particularly as we see in Esther 4:11. In this verse, Esther hesitates to approach King Xerxes because she knows the danger involved. The law in the Persian empire was clear—anyone, man or woman, who entered the king's inner court without being summoned faced the death penalty unless the king extended his golden scepter to spare their life. This fear is not unfounded; it's based on a very real threat that could lead to her death. Esther is not a superhuman figure without fear—she is just like us. She has doubts, she is scared, and she knows that what Mordecai is asking of her could cost her everything. But it's in this hesitation and fear that we learn one of the most profound lessons of the story: courage is not the absence of fear, but the willingness to act despite it.

At this moment in the story, Esther is caught between two conflicting forces. On one hand, she is deeply aware of the life-threatening risk involved in going before the king uninvited. On the other hand, she feels the growing weight of responsibility that Mordecai has placed on her shoulders to save her people. The fear she experiences is not irrational—it is completely justified. Yet, what makes Esther's story so powerful is how she moves from this place of fear to a place of action and bravery. Her fear motivates her to carefully weigh the cost of her choices, and it leads her to a moment of deep reflection. Sometimes, fear can paralyze us, making us feel powerless to act. But in Esther's case, her fear becomes a catalyst for deeper thought, for prayer, and for seeking God's guidance. She does not ignore her fear; she faces it head-on, and in doing so, she finds the strength to act.

In our own lives, we often face moments where fear threatens to hold us back from doing what we know is right. Whether it's the fear of failure, rejection, or even personal loss, fear can be a powerful motivator, either pushing us toward action or holding us back in inaction. The fear Esther felt was the fear of death—a fear most of us will hopefully never have to experience to the same degree. But her story reminds us that no matter how intense our fear may be, we can find the courage to do what is right. Esther's hesitation is a reminder that even the greatest heroes in history were not fearless—they were simply courageous enough to act in spite of their fear.

As Esther wrestles with her decision, she is reminded by Mordecai that the fate of the Jewish people rests in her hands. His words are not easy to hear, and they place an immense burden on Esther's shoulders. She knows that if she chooses to remain silent, the destruction of her people is almost certain. But even with this knowledge, the fear of approaching the king uninvited is still very real. Esther's story teaches us that it is okay to feel afraid when faced with overwhelming situations. Fear is a natural response to danger and uncertainty, but it doesn't have to control our actions. In fact, it is often in overcoming fear that we find the courage to make the most important choices of our lives.

The law in Persia at the time was absolute, and no one could simply walk into the king's presence without being summoned. Esther knew that even though she was queen, she was not exempt from this law. This is an important detail in the story because it shows that Esther's position of power did not protect her from the consequences of her actions. She was not immune to the risks, and she was fully aware of what could happen if the king did not show her favor. The fact that she hadn't been called to see the king in thirty days only added to her anxiety. Would the king even want to see her? Would he extend his scepter and spare her life, or would her boldness lead to her death? These were real questions that must have plagued Esther's mind as she weighed her options.

In this moment of fear and hesitation, we see Esther's humanity. She is not depicted as a fearless warrior who charges into battle without a second thought. Instead, she is shown as a thoughtful, reflective, and cautious individual who understands the weight of the decision before her. This makes Esther a relatable figure for us today. We too face moments in our lives where the stakes are high, and the consequences of our choices could be life-altering. Whether it's standing up for what is right in the face of opposition, taking a leap of faith in our careers, or making a personal sacrifice for the sake of others, we are often called to act with courage even when fear is present.

The lesson we learn from Esther's fear is that courage is not about being fearless; it's about acting despite the fear. Esther did not deny or downplay the danger she was facing. She acknowledged it fully, but she also recognized that her fear could not dictate her actions. As she moves forward in the story, we see how she overcomes her fear through a combination of prayer, reflection, and ultimately, faith. Her decision to fast and ask others to join her in fasting shows that she understood the gravity of the situation and knew that she could not face it alone. This period of fasting was not just a way for Esther to prepare herself mentally and emotionally; it was also an act of faith, a way of seeking God's guidance and protection in a moment of great uncertainty.

When we face fear in our own lives, it's important to remember that we don't have to face it alone either. Just as Esther sought support from those around her, we too can lean on our communities, our faith, and our loved ones for strength and encouragement. Esther's willingness to fast and pray also reminds us of the importance of seeking spiritual guidance when making difficult decisions. In moments of fear and uncertainty, turning to God can provide us with the peace and clarity we need to move forward with courage.

One of the most powerful moments in the story comes when Esther finally resolves to go before the king. Her words, "If I perish, I perish," (Esther 4:16) reflect a deep acceptance of the risk involved and a willingness to lay down her life if necessary. This statement is not one of despair, but of determination. It shows that Esther has reached a point where her fear no longer controls her. Instead, she is motivated by a sense of duty and responsibility to her people. She knows that the risk is great, but she also knows that the cost of inaction is even greater. Her willingness to face death for the sake of others is a testament to her selflessness and bravery.

Esther's courageous choice to approach the king, despite the fear of death, is a reminder to all of us that sometimes the greatest acts of courage come when we are willing to sacrifice our own safety for the sake of others. Whether it's standing up for a friend, defending the rights of the marginalized, or speaking out against injustice, we are often called to put aside our own fears and take action for the greater good. Esther's story challenges us to think about the ways in which we can use our own positions of influence, no matter how big or small, to make a difference in the world around us.

In today's world, we are faced with countless opportunities to act courageously in the face of fear. Whether it's standing up for our beliefs, advocating for those who are vulnerable, or simply doing what is right in difficult situations, we all have moments where fear threatens to hold us back. Esther's story reminds us that courage doesn't mean the absence of fear—it means choosing to act even when we are afraid. Her willingness to step into the unknown, to risk her life for the sake of her people, is a powerful example of what it means to lead with bravery and conviction.

In conclusion, Esther's Motivation through Fear is a powerful reminder that courage often requires us to face our fears head-on. Her initial hesitation to approach the king reflects the very real danger she faced, but it also highlights the inner struggle that many of us experience when we are called to make difficult choices. The fear of failure, rejection, or personal loss can be overwhelming, but Esther's story teaches us that we cannot let fear dictate our actions. Instead, we must acknowledge our fear, seek guidance, and ultimately, act with courage. Esther's willingness to say, "If I perish, I perish," shows that true courage comes from accepting the risks involved and moving forward with faith. Her story challenges us to think about how we respond to fear in our own lives. Will we allow it to paralyze us, or will we use it as motivation to take bold and courageous action? Just as Esther overcame her fear to save her people, we too can find the strength to act with courage, even in the face of our greatest fears.

Chapter 4 - Mordecai's Challenge

In the story of Esther, one of the pivotal moments that showcases her courage is found in Mordecai's Challenge in Esther 4:14. This verse represents a turning point in the narrative, both for Esther as an individual and for the fate of the Jewish people. Mordecai, her cousin and mentor, issues a challenge that cuts straight to the heart of Esther's dilemma. He tells her, "For if thou altogether holdest thy peace at this time, then shall there enlargement and deliverance arise to the Jews from another place; but thou and thy father's house shall be destroyed: and who knoweth whether thou art come to the kingdom for such a time as this?" This powerful message from Mordecai is not just a call to action, but a reminder of the heavy responsibility that rests on Esther's shoulders. It is a challenge that forces Esther to confront the reality of her position, her power, and her purpose. Up until this point, Esther has hesitated to act, knowing that approaching the king without being summoned could mean her death. But now, Mordecai's words push her to realize that silence in the face of such evil is not an option. His challenge is clear: if Esther remains silent, God's deliverance for the Jewish people will come from elsewhere, but she and her family will not escape the consequences of inaction.

This challenge is both sobering and motivating. Mordecai is not simply trying to convince Esther to act out of fear for her own safety; he is urging her to recognize that she has been placed in a unique position of influence for a reason. His famous line, "Who knoweth whether thou art come to the kingdom for such a time as this?" is a profound statement that underscores the idea of divine purpose. Mordecai is challenging Esther to see that her rise to the position of queen is not a coincidence or a stroke of luck. She has been placed in this role at this specific time for a reason, and that reason is now unfolding before her. The fate of an entire people hangs in the balance, and Esther's choice—to act or to remain silent—will determine the outcome. Mordecai's challenge to Esther is a reminder that there are moments in life when we are called to step into our purpose, even when the risks are great.

For Esther, this challenge forces her to grapple with the idea of responsibility. As queen, she holds a position of power and influence, but that power comes with a responsibility to use it for the greater good. Mordecai's challenge highlights the fact that positions of influence are not given to us for our own benefit or comfort; they are given to us so that we can make a difference in the world around us. This is a lesson that resonates deeply with us today. Whether we hold positions of authority in our jobs, our communities, or our families, we all have the ability to influence those around us. But with that influence comes the responsibility to stand up for what is right, to speak out against injustice, and to use our voices to advocate for those who cannot speak for themselves. Mordecai's challenge to Esther is a call to courage—not just for her, but for all of us. It is a reminder that silence in the face of evil brings consequences, but courage can lead to deliverance.

Mordecai's words also carry a message of hope. He tells Esther that if she chooses not to act, deliverance for the Jewish people will still come from another place. This statement reflects Mordecai's faith in God's sovereignty. He believes that God's plan for the Jewish people will not be thwarted, even if Esther chooses not to be a part of it. This is an important lesson for all of us: God's plans are not dependent on any one person. However, we are given the opportunity to be part of those plans, to play a role in bringing about God's deliverance and justice in the world. Mordecai's challenge to Esther is an invitation to participate in something much bigger than herself. It is an invitation to be a vessel for God's work, to be the person through whom deliverance comes. This message is incredibly empowering, as it reminds us that we have the ability to make a difference, even in situations that seem overwhelming or impossible.

At the same time, Mordecai's challenge is a stark warning. He tells Esther that if she chooses to remain silent, she and her family will not escape the consequences. This part of the message is a reminder that inaction in the face of evil has its own set of consequences. Esther may have been tempted to believe that by staying quiet and blending into the background, she could protect herself and avoid the risks associated with confronting the king. But Mordecai makes it clear that silence is not a safe option. In fact, it is the most dangerous choice she could make. This warning is a powerful reminder that there are times in life when silence is not neutral. When we choose not to speak out against injustice or to stand up for what is right, we are not simply avoiding conflict—we are allowing evil to flourish unchecked. Mordecai's challenge to Esther is a call to recognize that silence in the face of evil is, in itself, a form of complicity. And just as Esther would not escape the consequences of her silence, neither do we when we choose to remain passive in the face of wrongdoing.

The story of Esther's courageous choice in response to Mordecai's challenge is a timeless lesson in bravery, responsibility, and faith. Esther's initial hesitation is understandable—after all, she was facing a life-or-death situation. But Mordecai's challenge pushes her to look beyond her fear and to recognize the greater purpose for which she has been placed in her position. His words inspire her to take a step of faith, to trust that God has placed her in this moment for a reason, and to act with courage in the face of overwhelming odds. When Esther finally resolves to go before the king, knowing full well the risks involved, she embodies the kind of bravery that we are all called to display in our own lives.

Esther's story is not just about one woman's courageous choice; it is a story about how ordinary people can make extraordinary differences when they choose to act with courage. Esther was not born into royalty, nor was she trained to be a leader. She was a young Jewish woman who found herself thrust into a position of power at a critical moment in history. Her story reminds us that we do not have to be born into privilege or have all the right qualifications to make a difference. What matters is our willingness to step up when the moment calls for it. Like Esther, we may find ourselves in situations where we are the only ones with the ability to speak out or to take action. And like Esther, we may be filled with fear and doubt about whether we are capable of making a difference. But Mordecai's challenge reminds us that we are not placed in these situations by accident. We are called to these moments for a reason, and we have a responsibility to act.

The story of Esther also highlights the importance of faith in times of crisis. Mordecai's challenge to Esther reflects his deep faith in God's plan, even when the situation seems hopeless. He believes that God will deliver the Jewish people, whether through Esther or someone else. This faith is a source of strength for Esther as she grapples with her decision. It reminds her that she is not acting alone; God is with her, guiding her steps and using her to bring about deliverance. This is a powerful lesson for all of us. When we face difficult choices or overwhelming challenges, we can take comfort in the knowledge that we are not alone. God is at work in our lives, even when we cannot see it, and He has a purpose for us in every situation we face.

In conclusion, Mordecai's Challenge to Esther in Esther 4:14 is a pivotal moment that pushes her to move from a place of fear and hesitation to a place of courage and action. His words remind her that silence in the face of evil brings consequences, but courage can lead to deliverance. Mordecai's challenge is not just for Esther—it is a challenge for all of us. It is a call to recognize the moments in our lives when we are placed in positions of influence for a reason, and to use that influence to stand up for what is right. It is a reminder that inaction is not a neutral choice; it has its own set of consequences. And it is an invitation to be part of something bigger than ourselves, to step into our purpose, and to trust that God is with us every step of the way. Esther's courageous choice to heed Mordecai's challenge and to risk her life for the sake of her people is a powerful example of what it means to act with bravery, responsibility, and faith. Her story continues to inspire us to face our own challenges with the same courage, knowing that we are called to these moments for such a time as this.

Chapter 5 - Moment of Decision

In the story of Esther, the Moment of Decision comes in Esther 4:16, where she famously declares, "If I perish, I perish." This statement, brief but powerful, marks the turning point in Esther's journey from a young woman thrust into royal power to a courageous leader willing to risk everything for the sake of her people. At this moment, Esther is no longer hiding in the comfort of the palace, nor is she hesitating under the weight of fear. Instead, she steps boldly into her role, accepting the danger that lies ahead. Her words, "If I perish, I perish," are not spoken out of despair, but out of resolve and faith. It is a declaration of determination, one that shows she has fully accepted the consequences of her actions, no matter what they may be. This moment of decision is what defines Esther's courage, for it is not the absence of fear that makes her brave, but the fact that she chooses to act despite the fear. She knows the risks, yet she chooses to do what is right anyway. This is true courage.

Esther's decision to go before the king without being summoned is a life-threatening choice. According to Persian law, anyone who approached the king without his invitation could be put to death, unless the king extended his golden scepter in mercy. For Esther, this was no small matter. She had not been summoned by the king for thirty days, and there was no guarantee that she would find favor with him. Approaching the king meant walking directly into the possibility of her own death. But Esther's words, "If I perish, I perish," show that she has reached a place of complete surrender. She has decided that the safety of her people is worth more than her own life. This is a profound moment of selflessness. Esther is no longer thinking about her own comfort or survival—she is thinking about the greater good, about the lives of her fellow Jews who are under the threat of annihilation. In this moment, she takes on the role of an intercessor, willing to put her own life on the line to save others.

The lesson from Esther's moment of decision is one that resonates deeply with all of us. We all face moments in life where we must make difficult decisions—decisions that come with risks, that challenge our comfort, and that may even demand personal sacrifice. Esther's story reminds us that true courage is found in the willingness to act in the face of danger. Courage is not about being fearless; it is about moving forward despite fear. Esther shows us that when the stakes are high, when the lives of others are at risk, we must be willing to take bold action, even if it means facing uncertainty or peril. Her famous declaration, "If I perish, I perish," is a reminder that some things are worth fighting for, even if the outcome is uncertain.

Esther's moment of decision also teaches us about the power of faith. Before she makes her decision, Esther calls for a time of fasting and prayer, asking all the Jews in the city to join her in seeking God's guidance. This shows that her decision to approach the king is not made lightly or impulsively. It is made after deep reflection, prayer, and seeking the wisdom of God. Esther's courage is not rooted in her own strength, but in her faith in God's providence. She believes that God has placed her in this position for a reason, and she is willing to step into that purpose, trusting that whatever happens, God is in control. This is an important lesson for all of us. When we face difficult decisions, especially those that come with great risk, it is vital that we seek God's guidance and trust in His plan. Esther's decision shows us that even in the face of uncertainty, we can move forward with courage when we place our trust in God.

Another key lesson from Esther's moment of decision is the importance of taking responsibility. Up until this point in the story, Esther has been somewhat passive, following the advice of Mordecai and navigating her role in the palace. But in this moment, she takes full responsibility for the fate of her people. She understands that she is in a unique position to make a difference, and she chooses to step into that responsibility, even though it comes with great personal risk. This is a powerful example of leadership. True leaders are willing to take responsibility, even when the cost is high. Esther could have chosen to remain silent, to protect herself, and to stay safe within the walls of the palace. But she recognizes that her silence would come at a greater cost—the lives of her people. In this moment of decision, Esther shows us that leadership is not about self-preservation; it is about putting the needs of others before your own. It is about taking action, even when that action comes with great risk.

Esther's story also challenges us to think about how we respond to moments of crisis in our own lives. When faced with difficult choices, do we retreat in fear, or do we step forward in faith? Esther's decision to approach the king, knowing full well that she might perish, is a reminder that sometimes we are called to take risks for the sake of others. We are called to be courageous, even when we don't know what the outcome will be. Esther's words, "If I perish, I perish," show that she is willing to accept whatever consequences come from her actions, because she knows that doing the right thing is more important than preserving her own life. This is a lesson that we can apply to our own lives. There are times when we must be willing to take risks, to step out in faith, and to do what is right, even when the outcome is uncertain.

In today's world, we are often faced with situations that require courage. Whether it's standing up for justice, defending the rights of the vulnerable, or speaking out against wrongdoing, we are called to be like Esther—to act with courage, even when it's hard. Esther's moment of decision reminds us that we all have a role to play in making the world a better place. We may not be queens or kings, but we all have influence in our own circles, and we all have the ability to make a difference. Esther's story challenges us to think about how we can use our influence to help others, to stand up for what is right, and to take bold action when it is needed.

Another important aspect of Esther's moment of decision is the theme of identity. Throughout the story, Esther has hidden her Jewish identity from the king and from those around her in the palace. But in this moment, she is forced to confront who she really is. By choosing to approach the king on behalf of her people, Esther is choosing to reveal her true identity as a Jew. This is a significant moment, because it shows that Esther is no longer hiding or pretending to be someone she's not. She is fully embracing who she is and is willing to stand up for her people, even if it means risking her life. This is a powerful lesson for all of us. There are times in life when we must stop hiding who we are, when we must stand up and be counted, and when we must fully embrace our identity, even if it comes with risks. Esther's decision to reveal her true identity in order to save her people is a reminder that we cannot hide from who we are. We must be willing to stand in our truth, even when it's difficult.

Esther's declaration, "If I perish, I perish," is a moment of profound bravery, but it is also a moment of great faith. By making this decision, Esther is putting her life in God's hands, trusting that whatever happens, He will be with her. This level of trust and surrender is something that we can all learn from. In our own lives, we are often faced with situations where we don't know what the outcome will be. We may be afraid of what will happen if we take a certain step or make a certain decision. But Esther's story reminds us that we can trust God with the unknown. We can move forward with courage, knowing that He is in control, and that He will guide us through whatever challenges we face.

In conclusion, Esther's Moment of Decision in Esther 4:16 is a powerful example of true courage. Her famous declaration, "If I perish, I perish," shows that she is willing to risk her life for the sake of her people, and that she has fully accepted the consequences of her actions. This moment is a turning point in Esther's story, as she moves from hesitation and fear to bold action and faith. The lessons we learn from Esther's decision are profound. She teaches us that courage is not the absence of fear, but the willingness to act despite it. She shows us the importance of faith, responsibility, and selflessness. She challenges us to take risks for the greater good, to stand up for what is right, and to trust God with the outcome. Esther's moment of decision is a reminder that we all face moments in life where we must choose to act with courage, even when the stakes are high. Like Esther, we must be willing to step forward in faith, to take responsibility for the influence we have, and to use that influence to make a difference in the world.

Chapter 6 - Mobilizing for Support

In the story of Esther, one of the most powerful themes is Mobilizing for Support, which comes to the forefront in Esther 4:16 when she says, "Go, gather together all the Jews that are present in Shushan, and fast ye for me..." This verse represents Esther's recognition that she cannot face the immense challenge ahead of her alone. At this point in the narrative, she is preparing to risk her life by going before King Xerxes without being summoned, a move that could result in her death. But before she takes this bold and dangerous step, Esther does something incredibly important—she calls upon the collective support of her people. She doesn't just rely on her own strength, but seeks the strength of her community through fasting and prayer. This moment is significant because it shows Esther's understanding that true courage and success are not born out of individual efforts alone, but through the collective faith and unity of those around us. Esther's call to gather the Jews in fasting and prayer emphasizes the power of communal support, especially in times of great danger.

This act of mobilizing for support is not just about seeking emotional encouragement; it is a deeply spiritual action. Esther recognizes the spiritual weight of the task ahead of her and knows that she needs God's guidance and protection. Fasting, in this context, is a way of humbling oneself before God, seeking His will, and demonstrating dependence on His strength rather than relying solely on human ability. Esther's decision to ask the Jews in the city of Shushan to fast for her shows her humility and her understanding that this situation is far beyond what she can handle on her own. It is an acknowledgment that, while she is the one who must physically go before the king, the outcome is ultimately in God's hands. By calling for a fast, Esther invites her people to join her in seeking divine intervention, creating a sense of solidarity and shared responsibility in the face of danger.

The lesson we learn from Esther's decision to mobilize support is a powerful one. In our own lives, we often face challenges that feel overwhelming, and it can be tempting to try to tackle them on our own. We may think that asking for help is a sign of weakness, or that we need to prove our strength by handling things independently. But Esther's story teaches us that there is great strength in seeking the support of others, particularly when we face moments of crisis. Fasting and prayer, in this context, represent not just a religious practice, but a way of uniting people in a common cause. By mobilizing her community to fast and pray, Esther is showing that she values the power of collective faith. She knows that the prayers of her people can move mountains, and she is not afraid to ask for their help. This is a crucial lesson for us today: when we face difficult or dangerous situations, we don't have to go through them alone. There is power in community, in shared faith, and in collective prayer.

Esther's request for fasting and prayer is also a sign of her leadership. True leadership is not about going it alone or always having the answers—it's about recognizing when you need the support and wisdom of others. By asking the Jewish community to fast with her, Esther is exercising a form of leadership that is grounded in humility and reliance on God. She understands that, as the queen, she has a unique role to play, but she also knows that her success depends on the prayers and support of her people. This is a valuable lesson in leadership for all of us. Whether we are in positions of authority or not, we all face times when we need the wisdom and strength that comes from seeking support from others. Esther's willingness to ask for help shows that she is not trying to be a hero on her own—she is leading by bringing her people together in a united effort to seek God's intervention.

Fasting, as mentioned in Esther 4:16, is a way of focusing the mind and heart on God. It is an act of sacrifice, a way of setting aside physical needs to concentrate on spiritual ones. By asking the Jews to fast, Esther is calling them to put their trust in God completely. This fasting was not just for Esther's success, but for the survival of the entire Jewish people. Esther's act of mobilizing for support through fasting shows that the battle she is about to face is not merely a political or personal one—it is a spiritual battle. And in this battle, she needs the strength that comes from collective prayer and fasting. The Jews in Shushan, by joining Esther in fasting, are participating in this spiritual struggle. They are not just bystanders; they are actively engaged in seeking God's mercy and protection.

The act of fasting also serves as a way for Esther to prepare herself for the enormous task ahead. Fasting is often used as a way to seek clarity and guidance, and by calling for a fast, Esther is making sure that she is spiritually and mentally prepared for the dangers she will face. She is about to make one of the most significant decisions of her life, and she knows that she needs to be fully aligned with God's will. Fasting helps her focus, strip away distractions, and place her trust in God's plan. In our own lives, we can learn from Esther's example by recognizing the importance of preparation, both spiritually and mentally, before taking on great challenges. Esther's call for fasting shows that she is not rushing into a dangerous situation without thought; she is carefully preparing herself, her mind, and her spirit for the task ahead.

Esther's decision to mobilize support through fasting also highlights the importance of unity in times of crisis. By gathering the Jewish community to fast and pray, Esther is bringing people together around a common cause. In times of danger or uncertainty, there is great power in unity. The collective strength of a community bound by a shared purpose can accomplish far more than any one individual acting alone. Esther's leadership brings her people together in a time of desperation, and together they seek God's intervention. This lesson is especially relevant today, as we live in a world where division and isolation are common. Esther's story reminds us that in moments of crisis, we are stronger together. When we face difficulties, we should not be afraid to reach out to others, to unite around a common purpose, and to seek support from our communities.

The communal nature of Esther's fast also reflects the interconnectedness of the Jewish people. Esther's fate is tied to the fate of her people, and by fasting together, the Jewish community is showing that they are all in this together. They are not just fasting for Esther—they are fasting for their own survival. This collective action builds a sense of solidarity, reminding the Jewish people that their destinies are intertwined. This is an important lesson for us today, as we often face challenges that affect not just ourselves, but our families, friends, and communities. Esther's story encourages us to recognize the ways in which our actions impact others and to seek communal support when we face difficult decisions.

Another key aspect of Esther's request for fasting is that it involves all the Jews in Shushan. This is not just a personal, private fast for Esther—it is a communal act of faith. By asking everyone to participate, Esther is creating a sense of shared responsibility. The outcome of her actions will affect the entire Jewish population, and she wants everyone to be involved in seeking God's guidance. This shows the power of collective prayer. When a community comes together in faith, the impact can be transformative. Esther's request for communal fasting teaches us that there is strength in numbers, especially when those numbers are united in prayer and faith.

In conclusion, Esther's decision to Mobilize for Support in Esther 4:16 is a powerful example of the importance of community, faith, and collective action in times of danger and crisis. Her request for fasting and prayer shows that she understands the spiritual weight of the situation and that she cannot face it alone. By gathering the Jews in Shushan to fast with her, Esther is demonstrating the power of communal support and the strength that comes from collective faith. This moment in the story reminds us that we do not have to face challenges on our own; there is power in seeking the support of others, especially through prayer and fasting. Esther's leadership in this moment is grounded in humility and reliance on God, and her decision to seek the prayers of her community shows that true courage often comes from recognizing that we cannot do it all by ourselves. Esther's story teaches us that in times of crisis, we must be willing to reach out to others, to unite in faith, and to seek God's guidance together. This powerful lesson is as relevant today as it was in Esther's time, reminding us that we are stronger together, especially when we stand united in faith and prayer.

Chapter 7 - Moving in Faith

In the story of Esther, her Moving in Faith is beautifully captured in Esther 5:1, where the verse reads, "Now it came to pass on the third day, that Esther put on her royal apparel, and stood in the inner court of the king's house." This simple act of stepping into the inner court might seem ordinary at first glance, but in reality, it represents one of the most profound moments of faith and courage in the entire narrative. Esther had spent days in fasting and prayer, preparing herself spiritually and mentally for this exact moment. Now, the time had come for her to act. The stakes couldn't have been higher—approaching King Xerxes without an invitation was against Persian law, and the penalty for doing so was death, unless the king extended his scepter in an act of mercy. Esther was well aware of the risks, yet she chose to move forward in faith, trusting that God would guide her and that her actions would result in the salvation of her people. This moment of decision, when she put on her royal robes and walked into the king's court, is not just about bravery—it is about her absolute reliance on God's providence as she steps into the unknown with both courage and grace.

Esther's choice to approach the king reflects the depth of her faith. She didn't know how the king would respond. She didn't have any guarantees that he would show her favor. All she knew was that her people's lives depended on her willingness to act, and so she moved forward, despite the uncertainty, despite the fear. This is the essence of moving in faith—acting even when the outcome is unclear, trusting that God will make a way where there seems to be no way. For Esther, her faith wasn't passive; it was active, demonstrated through her willingness to take a risk that could have cost her everything. The fact that she put on her royal apparel for this moment is significant as well. She understood the power of presentation, and she knew that appearing before the king in her full royal attire would remind him of her position and significance. But more than that, putting on her royal clothes was a symbolic act. It signified that Esther was stepping fully into the role she had been given as queen. She wasn't hiding in fear or shrinking back—she was embracing her identity and the responsibility that came with it. Her royal apparel was not just a costume; it was a declaration that she was ready to face whatever came next with dignity and faith.

This act of faith by Esther serves as a powerful lesson for all of us today. In our own lives, we are often called to step into situations where the outcome is uncertain. We face decisions that come with risks, and we are required to move forward, even when we don't know how things will turn out. Esther's story teaches us that faith is not about having all the answers or knowing exactly what will happen—it's about trusting in God's plan and being willing to take that first step, even when the path ahead is unclear. Esther didn't wait for everything to be perfectly lined up before she acted. She didn't wait for a sign from the king or for a guarantee of safety. She moved forward in faith, believing that God had placed her in this position for a reason and that He would guide her through whatever challenges she faced. This is a reminder to all of us that faith often requires action. It's not enough to simply believe that God is in control—we must be willing to move forward in that belief, trusting that He will direct our steps as we go.

Esther's approach to the king also highlights the importance of grace under pressure. She didn't rush into the king's presence recklessly or in a state of panic. Instead, she approached with calmness, grace, and dignity. This shows the balance between courage and wisdom. Esther understood the gravity of the situation, and she prepared herself accordingly. Her faith didn't lead her to act impulsively; it led her to act thoughtfully and strategically. This is an important lesson for us as well. Faith doesn't mean acting without thought or consideration—it means trusting God's plan while also using the wisdom and discernment He has given us. Esther's grace under pressure is a powerful example of how we can move forward in difficult situations with both courage and composure.

Another key aspect of this moment is the fact that Esther waited three days before approaching the king. These three days were spent in fasting and prayer, both for herself and for her people. This period of waiting is significant because it shows that Esther didn't rush into action without seeking God's guidance first. She understood the importance of preparation—spiritual, mental, and emotional preparation. Before taking on such a dangerous and monumental task, Esther sought the strength and wisdom that comes from spending time in

God's presence. This is a crucial lesson for us as well. When we face difficult or uncertain situations, it's important to take time to pray, reflect, and seek God's guidance before moving forward. Esther's willingness to wait and prepare shows that faith is not just about action—it's also about knowing when to pause, seek God's will, and then move forward with clarity and purpose.

Esther's decision to approach the king also highlights the theme of identity. Throughout the story, Esther had concealed her Jewish identity from those in the palace. But in this moment, as she moves forward in faith, she is no longer hiding who she is. By choosing to stand up for her people, Esther is fully embracing her identity as a Jewish woman, even though it puts her at risk. This is a powerful reminder that moving in faith often requires us to fully embrace who we are, even when it's difficult or dangerous. Esther's willingness to reveal her true identity in order to save her people shows that faith involves being honest and authentic, even when it comes at a cost. In our own lives, we may face situations where we are tempted to hide parts of ourselves or to avoid standing up for what we believe in. But Esther's story reminds us that true courage and faith come from being true to who we are and standing up for what is right, even when it's risky.

Esther's approach to the king also reflects the idea of intercession. In this moment, Esther is not just acting on her own behalf—she is acting on behalf of her people. She is putting herself in harm's way in order to save others. This act of intercession is a powerful example of selflessness and courage. Esther is willing to risk her own life in order to plead for the lives of her fellow Jews. This is a reminder that faith is not just about personal gain or success—it's about being willing to sacrifice for the sake of others. Esther's willingness to intercede on behalf of her people shows that faith often involves standing in the gap for those who are in need, even when it comes at great personal risk. This is a lesson we can apply to our own lives, as we are often called to intercede for others, to stand up for those who are vulnerable, and to advocate for those who cannot speak for themselves.

The fact that Esther chose to move forward in faith, despite the risks, also shows her deep trust in God's providence. She didn't know what the outcome would be, but she trusted that God had a plan and that He would work things out according to His will. This is the essence of faith—trusting in God's plan even when we don't know what the future holds. Esther's story teaches us that we don't have to have all the answers in order to move forward. We just need to trust that

God is in control and that He will guide us as we take each step. This kind of faith requires a deep level of surrender, a willingness to let go of control and trust that God's plan is bigger and better than anything we could imagine. Esther's decision to approach the king is a powerful example of this kind of surrender and trust.

In conclusion, Esther's Moving in Faith in Esther 5:1 is a profound example of what it means to act with courage, grace, and trust in God's plan. Her decision to approach the king, knowing the risks involved, shows the depth of her faith and her willingness to act on behalf of her people. Esther didn't wait for everything to be perfectly lined up or for all the answers to be clear—she moved forward in faith, trusting that God would guide her steps. This is a powerful lesson for all of us. In our own lives, we are often called to step into situations where the outcome is uncertain, where the risks are high, and where we don't know exactly how things will turn out. But Esther's story reminds us that faith is not about having all the answers—it's about trusting God and being willing to take that first step. It's about moving forward, even when the path ahead is unclear, knowing that God is with us every step of the way. Esther's courage and grace in this moment serve as an example of what it means to move in faith, trusting that God will guide us through the challenges we face and that He will use our actions for His greater purpose. Just as Esther approached the king with faith and dignity, we too can move forward in our own lives with the same sense of trust, courage, and grace, knowing that God is in control and that He will see us through whatever challenges we face.

Chapter 8 - Merciful Favor

In the story of Esther, the theme of Merciful Favor is powerfully illustrated in Esther 5:2, where the verse reads, "And the king held out to Esther the golden scepter that was in his hand." This seemingly small gesture by King Xerxes is, in fact, a monumental moment that changes the course of history for the Jewish people. Esther had approached the king without being summoned, an act that could have cost her life, as Persian law dictated death for anyone who entered the king's presence uninvited—unless the king extended his golden scepter as a sign of mercy. For Esther, standing there in the inner court, this moment was filled with tension, fear, and uncertainty. She had stepped out in faith, risking her life for the sake of her people, and now everything hinged on whether the king would show her favor. When the king held out the golden scepter, it was not just a simple act of protocol—it was a profound moment of mercy and favor, a divine intervention that marked the turning point in Esther's courageous journey. It is in this act that we see how boldness and faith can unlock doors of favor, even in the most dire and dangerous situations.

Esther's approach to the king reflects the deep faith and courage she had cultivated over the previous days of fasting and prayer. She knew the risks, but she also knew that she couldn't remain silent while her people faced annihilation. So, with grace and bravery, she walked into the king's presence, fully aware that her life hung in the balance. The golden scepter represented her lifeline, her hope that the king would hear her plea and that her boldness would be rewarded with mercy. This act of mercy by the king is a powerful reminder of how God can work in unexpected ways, opening doors of favor and providing deliverance when we step out in faith. Esther's courage didn't guarantee a favorable outcome, but her willingness to act despite the risks opened the way for God's favor to manifest in her life.

The lesson from this moment is profound: boldness in faith often leads to favor in unexpected ways. Esther's decision to approach the king was not made lightly—she had spent days preparing spiritually through fasting and prayer, seeking God's guidance and wisdom. But even with all that preparation, there was no way for Esther to know how the king would respond. She had no assurance of safety, no promise that her boldness would be met with favor. Yet, she moved forward anyway, trusting that God was in control and that He would work through her actions. This is the essence of faith—acting without guarantees, stepping out in boldness when the outcome is uncertain, and trusting that God will provide what we need when we need it. For Esther, the king's extension of the golden scepter was the first sign that her boldness had unlocked favor, both with the king and with God.

In our own lives, we often face situations where we are called to step out in faith, to take bold actions even when we don't know how things will turn out. Like Esther, we may feel the weight of fear and uncertainty pressing down on us, wondering if our boldness will be met with favor or rejection. But Esther's story reminds us that when we move forward in faith, trusting in God's plan, we position ourselves to receive divine favor. The king's act of mercy was not something Esther could have predicted or controlled—it was an act of grace that came as a result of her willingness to take a risk for the greater good. This teaches us that favor is often found on the other side of boldness. When we are willing to step out, to act courageously, and to put our trust in God, we open the door for His mercy and favor to flow into our lives.

The golden scepter also symbolizes the power of grace and mercy. In this moment, King Xerxes held Esther's life in his hands, and with a simple gesture, he extended grace to her. This is a powerful image of how God's grace operates in our lives. Just as the king extended the scepter to Esther, sparing her life and allowing her to present her request, God extends His grace to us, inviting us into His presence and offering us favor that we do not deserve. Esther had no right to approach the king uninvited, just as we, in our own strength, have no right to approach a holy God. Yet, through His grace and mercy, God allows us to come before Him, to bring our requests, and to receive His favor. This is a reminder that God's favor is not something we can earn or manipulate—it is a gift that is given out of His love and grace. Esther's boldness was not about trying to manipulate the king or force her way into his presence. It was about trusting that

God would work through her actions and that, if it was His will, He would grant her favor. This is an important lesson for us as well: we cannot force God's hand or demand His favor, but when we move in faith and trust in His plan, He often responds with mercy and grace beyond what we could have imagined.

Esther's courageous approach to the king also demonstrates the importance of timing. She didn't rush into the king's presence impulsively or without preparation. She waited until the time was right, after days of fasting and prayer, and only then did she make her move. This shows the wisdom in waiting on God's timing, rather than acting out of fear or desperation. Esther understood that her boldness had to be coupled with patience and discernment. She knew that the situation was urgent, but she also knew that moving too quickly or without God's guidance could be disastrous. This is a lesson for all of us: faith and boldness are important, but so is waiting on God's perfect timing. When we rush ahead without seeking God's direction, we risk stepping outside of His will. But when we wait on His timing and move forward in faith, we often find that He has already prepared the way for us, just as He had prepared the king's heart to show favor to Esther.

The king's act of extending the golden scepter also reflects the importance of favor in positions of power. As queen, Esther had access to the king in a way that no one else did, but even her position as queen didn't guarantee her safety. It was the king's favor, not her title, that ultimately spared her life. This is a reminder that favor, not just power or position, is what often opens doors and brings success. Esther's boldness didn't come from her title or her status—it came from her faith in God and her willingness to step out in courage. And it was this faith that unlocked the favor she needed to fulfill her purpose. In our own lives, we may find ourselves in positions of influence or authority, but it is God's favor that ultimately determines our success. Esther's story reminds us that favor is a gift from God, and it often comes when we are willing to take risks and act with boldness and faith.

Another important aspect of this moment is the fact that Esther didn't just seek favor for herself—she was acting on behalf of her people. Her boldness wasn't driven by personal ambition or a desire for personal gain; it was motivated by her deep love and concern for the Jewish people, who were facing destruction. This teaches us that favor is not just about what we can receive for ourselves, but about how we can use the favor God grants us to bless others. Esther's courage in approaching the king was rooted in her desire to save her people, and it was this selflessness that made her boldness so powerful. In our own lives, we are often called to use the favor God grants us to help others, to stand up for those who are vulnerable, and to advocate for justice and mercy in our communities. Esther's story reminds us that when we act with boldness and faith on behalf of others, God often responds with favor and grace, opening doors that we could never open on our own.

The extension of the golden scepter also marks the beginning of a series of events that would ultimately lead to the deliverance of the Jewish people. This moment of favor set in motion a chain of events that would result in the downfall of Haman, the enemy who sought to destroy the Jews, and the salvation of Esther's people. This teaches us that small acts of favor can have far-reaching consequences. What might seem like a simple gesture—like the king extending the scepter—can be the turning point in a much larger plan. God often uses small moments of favor to bring about His greater purposes, and it is our responsibility to recognize those moments and move forward in faith. Esther's boldness in approaching the king unlocked a series of events that would lead to victory and deliverance, showing that when we step out in faith, God can use even the smallest moments of favor to bring about His plans.

In conclusion, Esther's experience of Merciful Favor in Esther 5:2 is a powerful example of how boldness and faith can unlock divine favor in dire situations. Her courageous approach to the king, despite the risks, was met with mercy and grace, showing that God often responds to our boldness with favor beyond what we could imagine. Esther's story teaches us that favor is not something we can earn or manipulate—it is a gift that comes when we trust in God's plan and move forward in faith. The king's extension of the golden scepter represents not only a moment of mercy but also the beginning of a greater plan for deliverance and salvation. Esther's boldness wasn't about personal gain—it was about saving her people, and it was this selflessness that made her actions so powerful. As we reflect on Esther's story, we are reminded that boldness in faith often leads to favor in unexpected ways, and that when we are willing to take risks for the sake of others, God often responds with mercy and

grace, opening doors we never thought possible. Esther's courageous approach to the king is a timeless reminder that when we move forward in faith, trusting in God's plan, we position ourselves to receive the favor and grace that only He can provide.

Chapter 9 - Making a Petition

The story of Esther is one of the most captivating accounts in the Bible, full of suspense, courage, and the ultimate triumph of good over evil. It takes place during a time when the Jewish people were living in exile in Persia, under the reign of King Ahasuerus (also known as Xerxes). Esther, a young Jewish woman, had risen to an unimaginable position—queen of Persia—after winning the king's favor in a beauty contest of sorts. But her rise to power was not without purpose. Though she may not have known it at first, Esther was placed in this position for a specific reason: to be the vessel through which her people would be saved. Esther's cousin Mordecai, who had raised her as his own daughter, played a pivotal role in her story as well. He was the one who first alerted her to the grave danger her people were in. Haman, a high-ranking official in the king's court, harbored a deep hatred for the Jews, particularly for Mordecai, because Mordecai refused to bow down to him. Out of his malice, Haman devised a sinister plot to have all the Jews in the kingdom annihilated. He manipulated the king into signing an edict that decreed the destruction of the Jews on a certain day. When Mordecai learned of this plan, he was devastated and immediately went into mourning. He wore sackcloth and ashes, a traditional sign of grief, and stood at the king's gate, crying out for his people. He sent word to Esther, urging her to go to the king and beg for mercy on behalf of her people. This was no small request, as approaching the king without being summoned was punishable by death, unless the king extended his golden scepter to the individual, granting them permission to speak. Esther knew the risks involved, and at first, she hesitated. But Mordecai's words to her were a powerful reminder of her purpose: "Who knoweth whether thou art come to the kingdom for such a time as this?" (Esther 4:14). These words stirred Esther's heart, and she realized that this was the moment for which she had been placed in her position of influence. She could not remain silent while her people faced annihilation. But Esther was not only courageous; she was also wise. She understood that simply bursting into the king's presence and pleading for her people might not yield the desired result. She needed to approach the situation with care, strategy, and patience. And so, she devised a plan. Esther asked Mordecai to gather all the Jews in the capital city of Shushan and have them fast for her for three days and three nights. She and her maidens would also fast. After this period of fasting and prayer, Esther was ready to make her move. On the third day, she dressed in her royal robes and approached the king's throne room. As she stood there, her heart must have been pounding with fear and anticipation. Would the king be pleased to see her, or would he be angered by her unbidden appearance? Thankfully, the king extended his golden scepter to her, inviting her to come forward and speak. Instead of immediately making her plea, Esther invited the king and Haman to a banquet that she had prepared for them. This was a brilliant move on her part. By inviting the king and Haman to a private banquet, she created an intimate setting where she could build rapport and gain favor. Esther's choice to delay her request also demonstrated her understanding of the importance of timing. She knew that the king needed to be in the right frame of mind to hear her petition, and that her request would have a greater impact if presented at the right moment. At the banquet, the king asked Esther what her request was, promising to grant it even up to half of his kingdom. Yet, once again, Esther held back. She did not make her petition known at that moment. Instead, she invited the king and Haman to a second banquet the following day. Esther's decision to wait until the second banquet to reveal her request shows her remarkable patience and strategic thinking. She was building up to her petition, ensuring that when she finally made her request, the king would be fully attentive and inclined to grant it. The fact that she waited not once, but twice, to present her petition, speaks volumes about her wisdom and her understanding of human nature. She knew that by delaying her request, she would create a sense of anticipation and curiosity in the king's mind, making him more likely to listen favorably when she finally revealed her true purpose. On the night between the two banquets, the king was unable to sleep, and he asked for the chronicles of the kingdom to be read to him. As the records were read, the king was reminded of how Mordecai had once uncovered a plot to assassinate him, but had never been rewarded for his loyalty. The timing of this revelation was no coincidence. God's hand was clearly at work, orchestrating the events that would lead to the deliverance of the Jewish people. The next day, at the second banquet, the king once again asked Esther what her request was. This time, Esther did not hold back. She revealed to the king that she and her people were in grave danger, and that Haman was the one responsible for plotting their destruction. The king was furious and immediately ordered that Haman be executed on the very gallows that he had prepared for Mordecai. Esther's petition had been granted, and her people were saved. The wisdom and courage that Esther displayed in making her petition are truly remarkable. She understood the importance of timing and strategy in pursuing justice. Instead of acting impulsively, she took the time to plan her approach carefully. She fasted and prayed, seeking God's guidance before taking action. She was patient, waiting for the right moment to present her request to the king. And when the time came, she spoke with clarity and conviction, revealing the truth and exposing the wickedness of Haman's plot. Esther's story teaches us several important lessons. First, it shows us the power of faith and prayer. Before making her petition, Esther sought God's guidance through fasting and prayer. She understood that she could not accomplish her mission on her own, but needed God's strength and wisdom to guide her. This is a powerful reminder that when we are faced with difficult decisions or overwhelming challenges, we should seek God's guidance through prayer, trusting that He will lead us in the right direction. Second, Esther's story teaches us the importance of patience and timing. Esther did not rush into her request, but waited for the right moment to act. She understood that timing was crucial, and that acting too soon or too late could jeopardize her mission. This is a valuable lesson for us as well. In our pursuit of justice or in any important endeavor, it is essential to be patient and discerning, waiting for the right moment to act. Sometimes, the best course of action is not to move forward immediately, but to wait, plan, and prepare, trusting that God will open the right doors at the right time. Third, Esther's story teaches us the importance of courage. Esther knew the risks involved in approaching the king, yet she did not let fear hold her back. She was willing to risk her own life to save her people. Her courage was not just in her willingness to face danger, but in her ability to remain calm and composed in the face of uncertainty. She trusted in God's plan and in her own instincts, and she did not let fear or desperation cloud her judgment. This is a powerful example for us to follow. Courage is not the absence of fear, but the willingness to act in spite of it. Finally, Esther's story teaches us the importance of using our influence for good.

Esther was placed in a position of power and influence for a reason. She could have remained silent and protected herself, but she chose to use her position to advocate for her people and to pursue justice. This is a reminder that when we are given influence, whether in our families, communities, or workplaces, we have a responsibility to use that influence for good, to speak up for those who cannot speak for themselves, and to stand up for what is right, even when it is difficult. In conclusion, Esther's courageous choice to make her petition to the king is a powerful example of faith, wisdom, patience, and courage. She shows us that true leadership and advocacy require not only boldness, but also discernment and strategy. Esther's story reminds us that in our own lives, when we are faced with challenges or opportunities to make a difference, we should seek God's guidance, wait for the right moment, and act with courage and conviction. Just as Esther's wise and courageous actions led to the salvation of her people, so too can our actions, when guided by faith and wisdom, bring about positive change in the world around us. Through Esther's example, we are encouraged to be brave in the face of adversity, to use our influence for good, and to trust that God will guide us in every step of the way.

Chapter 10 - Managing the Situation

In the story of Esther, we witness a moment of incredible courage, wisdom, and grace as she navigates a delicate and dangerous situation to save her people, the Jews, from annihilation. The backdrop of this story takes place in the kingdom of Persia, where Esther, a young Jewish woman, had risen to the position of queen, though her heritage was kept secret. At this time, Haman, a high-ranking official in the Persian court, harbored an intense hatred for the Jewish people, particularly for Esther's cousin Mordecai, who had refused to bow down to him. In his rage, Haman devised a plot to destroy all the Jews in the kingdom, convincing King Ahasuerus (also known as Xerxes) to issue an edict that decreed the annihilation of the Jewish people. Unbeknownst to the king, his beloved queen was herself Jewish, and this decree put her life, as well as the lives of her people, in mortal danger. Esther's position in the royal court gave her the unique opportunity to intervene on behalf of her people, but it also placed her in a precarious situation. To approach the king uninvited was to risk her life, as it was against the law to enter the king's presence without being summoned. However, Esther knew that she had to act, for the survival of her people depended on her. In Esther 7:3, we see the climax of her courageous choice, where she finally reveals her identity and makes her request known to the king, saying, "If I have found favor in thy sight, O king, and if it please the king, let my life be given me at my petition, and my people at my request." This moment is the culmination of Esther's careful and strategic management of the situation, and it highlights the immense wisdom she displayed in handling such a delicate matter. Esther's journey to this moment was not one of rash decisions or impulsive actions, but one of thoughtful consideration, patience, and reliance on divine guidance. When Mordecai first informed Esther of Haman's plot, she did not rush into the king's presence to plead for her people. Instead, she called for a three-day fast, during which she and the Jewish community of Shushan sought

God's guidance and intervention. This period of fasting was not only a spiritual preparation for Esther but also a time of reflection and planning. Esther understood that her approach to the king needed to be handled with the utmost care. After the fast, Esther put on her royal robes and approached the king's throne room, knowing full well the risk she was taking. When the king extended his golden scepter to her, inviting her to speak, Esther did not immediately reveal her request. Instead, she invited the king and Haman to a banquet that she had prepared. This was a calculated move on Esther's part, as she sought to create an intimate and favorable environment in which to present her case. At the first banquet, the king asked Esther what her petition was, promising to grant it even up to half of his kingdom. Yet, Esther chose to delay her request once again, inviting the king and Haman to a second banquet the following day. This decision to wait and build anticipation shows Esther's remarkable wisdom and her understanding of the importance of timing. By not rushing into her request, she ensured that the king's curiosity and interest were piqued, making him more likely to listen favorably when she finally revealed her true purpose. The second banquet marked the moment when Esther would reveal the truth. With the king and Haman seated before her, Esther carefully managed the situation, choosing her words with precision and tact. She began by appealing to the king's favor, acknowledging that her request was contingent upon his goodwill. "If I have found favor in thy sight, O king, and if it please the king," she began, humbly and respectfully. Esther understood the importance of maintaining the king's favor, and by framing her request in this way, she reminded him of the affection and esteem he had for her. This was not just a plea for justice; it was a personal appeal from the queen to the king, and Esther knew that the king's love for her would play a crucial role in the outcome of her petition. Next, Esther made her request: "Let my life be given me at my petition, and my people at my request." With these words, Esther revealed the gravity of the situation—that her very life, as well as the lives of her people, were at stake. Up until this moment, the king had been unaware of Esther's Jewish heritage, and thus, unaware that the decree he had signed would result in the death of his queen. Esther's choice to reveal her identity at this precise moment was a masterstroke of timing and strategy. She did not lead with this information, but rather waited until the right moment, when the king's favor was assured and when Haman's presence added weight to her revelation. In revealing her Jewish identity in this context, Esther managed the situation with great wisdom. She knew that the king's affection for her would cause him to react strongly to the idea that her life was in danger, and by extension, the lives of her people. Moreover, by making the request for her life and the lives of her people simultaneously, Esther skillfully connected her personal safety with the safety of the Jewish people, ensuring that the king would see the injustice of Haman's plot not just as a political or legal matter, but as a personal affront to him and his queen. Esther's approach in this moment is a powerful example of the value of wisdom and discernment in handling delicate situations. She did not rush to reveal the full extent of the danger, nor did she confront Haman directly in a public or confrontational manner. Instead, she created an environment in which the king was predisposed to listen favorably to her request, and she revealed the truth in a way that maximized the impact of her words. The way Esther managed this situation speaks to her deep understanding of human nature and the dynamics of power and influence. She knew that the king's emotional connection to her would play a critical role in his decision-making, and she used that connection to advocate not just for herself, but for her entire people. By framing her request in personal terms, Esther ensured that the king would feel a sense of urgency and responsibility to act. The outcome of Esther's courageous choice was nothing short of miraculous. The king, upon hearing Esther's plea and learning of Haman's treachery, was filled with rage. He ordered that Haman be executed on the very gallows that had been prepared for Mordecai, and the decree to destroy the Jews was overturned. Esther's careful management of the situation not only saved her own life but also the lives of countless others. In reflecting on Esther's story, we see that her courage was not just in the boldness of her actions, but in the wisdom with which she approached the situation. Esther understood the power of timing, the importance of maintaining favor, and the value of carefully choosing when and how to reveal the truth. Her story is a testament to the fact that courage and wisdom often go hand in hand, and that managing delicate situations requires not just boldness, but also patience, strategy, and discernment. Esther's example teaches us several important lessons that are relevant in our own lives. First, it shows us the importance of seeking divine guidance in times of difficulty. Before making her move, Esther called for a fast, seeking God's wisdom and intervention. This reminds us that in our own challenges, we should seek God's guidance and trust that He will provide the wisdom we need to navigate difficult situations. Second, Esther's story teaches us the value of patience and timing. Esther did not rush into her request, but waited for the right moment to act. She understood that timing was crucial, and that acting too soon could jeopardize her mission. This is a valuable lesson for us as well, as we often face situations where patience and discernment are needed to achieve the best outcome. Sometimes, the most courageous thing we can do is to wait and trust that the right moment will come. Third, Esther's story teaches us the importance of using our influence for good. Esther was in a unique position of power, and she chose to use that influence to advocate for her people. Her example reminds us that when we are in positions of influence or authority, we have a responsibility to use that influence to help others and to stand up for what is right. Finally, Esther's story teaches us the importance of wisdom in managing difficult situations. Esther did not act impulsively or recklessly, but instead carefully planned her approach, considering the best way to achieve her goal. Her wisdom in managing the situation was a key factor in her success, and it reminds us that when we face difficult situations, we too should seek to approach them with wisdom and discernment, rather than acting out of fear or haste. In conclusion, Esther's courageous choice to reveal her identity and make her petition to the king is a powerful example of faith, wisdom, and courage. Her careful management of the situation, from her initial fast to the moment of her revelation, demonstrates the value of patience, strategy, and divine guidance in handling delicate matters. Esther's story continues to inspire us today, reminding us that true courage is not just about bold action, but also about having the wisdom to navigate difficult situations with grace, patience, and trust in God's plan. Through her example, we are encouraged to seek God's guidance in our own challenges, to use our influence for good, and to approach difficult situations with wisdom and discernment, trusting that with God's help, we can achieve the best possible outcome.

Chapter 11 - Mordecai's Promotion

The story of Esther is one of the most remarkable accounts in the Bible, filled with themes of courage, faith, and divine intervention. Esther, a young Jewish woman, was thrust into the position of queen in a foreign land, Persia, at a time when her people faced great danger. The Persian king, Ahasuerus (also known as Xerxes), was unaware of her Jewish heritage when he chose her to be his queen, and this secret would later play a pivotal role in the salvation of her people. Esther's cousin, Mordecai, had raised her after the death of her parents, and he was a faithful servant of God, who refused to bow down to Haman, one of the king's highest officials. This act of defiance enraged Haman, who harbored a deep hatred for Mordecai and the Jewish people. In his wickedness, Haman devised a plot to destroy all the Jews in the kingdom, convincing the king to issue a decree that would lead to their annihilation. Unbeknownst to the king, this decree also meant the death of his beloved queen, Esther. Mordecai, upon learning of this plot, went into mourning and sent word to Esther, urging her to intercede on behalf of her people. However, approaching the king without being summoned was punishable by death unless the king extended his golden scepter, granting the person permission to speak. Esther was understandably afraid, but Mordecai's words stirred her heart. He reminded her that she may have been placed in her royal position "for such a time as this" (Esther 4:14), suggesting that God had orchestrated her rise to queen in order to save her people. After calling for a fast among the Jews, Esther gathered her courage and approached the king. Her bravery in this moment cannot be overstated, as she risked her life to save others. The king, moved by Esther's grace and courage, extended his golden scepter, sparing her life and allowing her to speak. Rather than immediately revealing her request, Esther wisely invited the king and Haman to a banquet, where she would later expose Haman's evil plot. This delay was not an act of hesitation but a display of strategic thinking, as Esther was waiting for the right moment to present her case. During the banquet, Esther revealed her Jewish identity and pleaded for her life and the lives of her people, exposing Haman as the architect of their impending destruction. The king, in a fit of rage upon learning of Haman's treachery, ordered that Haman be executed on the very gallows he had prepared for Mordecai. This was a dramatic turn of events, but the story does not end there. Esther's courage had saved her people from immediate danger, but the decree to destroy the Jews was still in place. According to Persian law, a royal edict could not be revoked, so a new plan had to be devised to counteract the previous decree. This is where we see the culmination of Esther's courage and faithfulness in the form of Mordecai's promotion, as described in Esther 8:2, where "the king took off his ring, which he had taken from Haman, and gave it unto Mordecai." This moment is significant not only because it represents the downfall of Haman and the elevation of Mordecai, but also because it highlights the divine justice that is at work throughout the entire story. Haman, who had sought to destroy Mordecai and the Jewish people, was now dead, and the very symbol of his authority—the king's ring—was given to Mordecai, the man he had despised. The king's ring was more than just a piece of jewelry; it was a symbol of power and authority. Whoever possessed the king's ring had the ability to act on behalf of the king, to make decrees, and to carry out the king's will. By giving this ring to Mordecai, the king was not only promoting him to a position of great power but was also reversing the evil that Haman had intended. Mordecai, a faithful servant of God, was now in a position to help deliver his people from the destruction that had been decreed against them. This reversal of fortune is a powerful demonstration of God's sovereignty and justice. Throughout the story, we see that even when evil seems to be prevailing, God is at work behind the scenes, orchestrating events for the good of His people. Esther's courage was the catalyst for this divine intervention, but Mordecai's promotion was the fulfillment of God's plan to bring about justice and deliverance. Mordecai's promotion also serves as a reminder that faithfulness, even in the face of adversity, can lead to divine elevation. Mordecai had remained steadfast in his refusal to bow down to Haman, even when it put his life at risk. He could have easily compromised his beliefs in order to save himself from Haman's wrath, but he chose to remain faithful to God, trusting that God would vindicate him in the end. And indeed, God did. Not only was Mordecai spared from death, but he was also elevated to a position of great power and influence, replacing the very man who had sought to destroy him. This promotion was not just a personal victory for Mordecai, but a victory for all the Jewish people. With Mordecai in a position of authority, he was able to work with Esther to devise a new plan to save their people. The king allowed Mordecai and Esther to issue a new decree that permitted the Jews to defend themselves against their enemies. When the appointed day of destruction arrived, the Jews were not slaughtered as Haman had planned, but instead, they triumphed over their enemies. This victory was a direct result of Esther's courageous choice to risk her life for her people and Mordecai's faithfulness in the face of adversity. The story of Esther and Mordecai teaches us that courage and faithfulness can lead to divine elevation and victory. Esther's bravery in approaching the king and revealing her identity was the turning point in the story, but it was her faithfulness to her people and her trust in God's plan that ultimately led to their salvation. Similarly, Mordecai's steadfastness in refusing to bow to Haman, despite the danger it posed to his life, was rewarded with promotion and power. Together, Esther and Mordecai demonstrate that when we remain faithful to God and act with courage in the face of adversity, God can use us to bring about great deliverance and victory, not just for ourselves, but for those around us. The lesson of Mordecai's promotion is also a reminder that God's timing is perfect. Throughout the story, there were moments when it seemed like evil was prevailing, when Haman's plot seemed unstoppable, and when the Jews faced certain destruction. But in the end, God's justice prevailed, and those who had been faithful were elevated to positions of honor and power. Mordecai's promotion came at the exact right time—after Esther's courageous actions had set the stage for deliverance, and after Haman's evil had been fully exposed. This teaches us that even when we cannot see how things will work out, we can trust that God is in control and that His timing is perfect. Mordecai's promotion also highlights the theme of divine justice. Haman had used his power and influence for evil, seeking to destroy an entire people out of his own pride and hatred. But in the end, his wickedness was his undoing, and the very position of power he had abused was given to the man he had sought to destroy. This reversal of fortune is a powerful reminder that God sees the injustices in the world, and He will bring about justice in His own time and in His own way. Mordecai's promotion was not just a personal vindication for him, but a demonstration of God's justice for all to see. The story of Esther and Mordecai is one of hope and encouragement for all who face difficult situations. It reminds us that even in the darkest of times, God is at work, and He can turn the tide in an instant. Esther's courage and Mordecai's faithfulness were the keys to their victory, but it was ultimately God who orchestrated the events that led to their deliverance. This teaches us that when we remain faithful to God and act with courage, we can trust that He will work all things together for our good. In conclusion, the promotion of Mordecai in Esther 8:2 is a powerful symbol of divine justice and elevation. Esther's courageous actions set the stage for Mordecai's rise to power, demonstrating that when we act with courage and faithfulness, God can bring about great deliverance and victory. Mordecai's promotion serves as a reminder that faithfulness, even in the face of adversity, can lead to divine elevation. It also teaches us that God's timing is perfect and that His justice will ultimately prevail. Through Esther's courage and Mordecai's faithfulness, we see the hand of God at work, bringing about justice and deliverance for His people. Their story continues to inspire us today, reminding us that when we remain faithful to God and act with courage, He can use us to bring about His purposes in the world. Just as Mordecai was promoted to a position of great power and influence, so too can God elevate us when we remain faithful to Him and trust in His plan.

Chapter 12 - Monumental Deliverance

The story of Esther is one of the most remarkable and inspiring narratives in the Bible, filled with powerful lessons about courage, faith, and the miraculous deliverance that can come from one brave choice. Esther, a young Jewish woman, became queen in Persia at a time when her people were living as a minority in a foreign land, surrounded by enemies. Though her rise to queenship might have seemed coincidental, it was all part of a divine plan, one that would require Esther to make a choice that would not only define her own life but also bring about monumental deliverance for her people. The verse in Esther 9:22—"As the days wherein the Jews rested from their enemies, and the month which was turned unto them from sorrow to joy, and from mourning into a good day"—beautifully captures the theme of transformation that runs throughout the entire story, showing how God can turn even the darkest and most hopeless situations into moments of victory, joy, and celebration. Esther's courageous choice to stand up for her people in the face of danger did not come easily, nor was it made without fear, but it resulted in a deliverance that not only saved lives but transformed a time of sorrow into a lasting legacy of joy and triumph for generations to come.

The story begins with King Ahasuerus (also known as Xerxes) ruling over a vast empire, which included many nations and peoples, including the Jews who had been exiled there from their homeland. After the king removed his former queen, Vashti, for refusing to appear at his banquet, he sought a new queen, and Esther, a Jewish woman, was chosen for her beauty and grace. However, her Jewish identity was kept a secret, and no one in the palace, not even the king, knew her true heritage. Esther's cousin, Mordecai, who had raised her after her parents died, was a faithful servant of God and played a pivotal role in the unfolding events. Mordecai, though a humble man, refused to bow to Haman, a high-ranking official in the king's court who was filled with pride and arrogance.

This act of defiance enraged Haman, and in his hatred for Mordecai, Haman devised a plan to destroy not just Mordecai but all the Jewish people living in the Persian Empire.

Haman's plot was sinister and far-reaching. He convinced the king to sign a decree that called for the destruction of all Jews on a specific day, casting lots—called "Pur"—to determine the exact day on which this genocide would occur. The Jews, scattered throughout the vast empire, were now living under the shadow of death, knowing that the day of their annihilation had been set. This decree was irrevocable, as Persian law could not be repealed once the king's seal had been placed upon it. The Jewish people were thrown into great mourning and despair, knowing that their days were numbered. Mordecai, upon hearing the decree, tore his clothes, put on sackcloth and ashes, and mourned publicly at the king's gate. His grief was not just personal but a reflection of the collective sorrow of the Jewish people, who faced imminent destruction.

Mordecai sent word to Esther, urging her to go before the king and plead for the lives of her people. But Esther faced a dilemma. Persian law was strict—no one, not even the queen, could approach the king without being summoned, and doing so could result in death unless the king extended his golden scepter as a sign of acceptance. Esther had not been called to the king in thirty days, and she knew that approaching him without being invited was a great risk. Fear gripped her, and she hesitated, knowing that her very life was at stake. But Mordecai's response to her hesitation was both powerful and prophetic. He reminded her that deliverance for the Jews would come, one way or another, because God's plan would not be thwarted, but he also challenged her with these stirring words: "And who knoweth whether thou art come to the kingdom for such a time as this?" (Esther 4:14). Mordecai's words were a reminder that Esther's rise to queenship was no accident—it was part of a divine purpose, and now was the time for her to act with courage.

With these words ringing in her ears, Esther made the fateful decision to risk her life and go before the king. But before doing so, she called for a three-day fast, asking Mordecai and all the Jews in the city of Shushan to join her in fasting and prayer. This period of fasting was not just a time of preparation but a demonstration of Esther's dependence on God for wisdom and strength. After the three days had passed, Esther dressed in her royal robes and stood in the inner court of the king's palace, waiting to see if the king would grant her an audience.

When King Ahasuerus saw her, he was pleased and extended his golden scepter, inviting her to speak. Esther had passed the first test—her life was spared, and she now had the opportunity to present her request.

But Esther, in her wisdom, did not immediately reveal her true purpose. Instead, she invited the king and Haman to a banquet she had prepared. This was a strategic move, as Esther knew the importance of timing and the need to create the right atmosphere for her petition. At the banquet, the king once again asked Esther what her request was, promising to grant her anything, even up to half of his kingdom. Yet Esther, sensing that the moment was not yet right, invited the king and Haman to a second banquet the following day. Esther's patience and discernment in waiting for the right moment to make her plea is a testament to her wisdom and understanding of the delicate nature of the situation.

At the second banquet, Esther finally revealed her true request to the king, saying, "If I have found favor in thy sight, O king, and if it please the king, let my life be given me at my petition, and my people at my request" (Esther 7:3). With these words, Esther not only revealed her Jewish identity but also exposed Haman's wicked plot to destroy her people. The king, shocked and enraged, immediately ordered that Haman be executed on the very gallows he had built for Mordecai. This dramatic reversal of fortune was a clear sign of divine justice, as the man who had plotted to destroy the Jews was himself destroyed.

But even with Haman's death, the decree to annihilate the Jews was still in effect, and Persian law could not be revoked. However, the king allowed Mordecai and Esther to issue a new decree, one that would allow the Jews to defend themselves against their enemies. This new decree was sent throughout the empire, and when the appointed day arrived, the Jews were ready to fight back. What had been intended as a day of destruction and sorrow was transformed into a day of victory and deliverance. The Jews triumphed over their enemies, and the day that had been set for their death became a day of joy and celebration.

The verse in Esther 9:22 reflects this incredible transformation: "As the days wherein the Jews rested from their enemies, and the month which was turned unto them from sorrow to joy, and from mourning into a good day..." This verse captures the essence of what Esther's courageous choice had accomplished. The Jewish people, who had been living under the threat of annihilation, were now at peace. Their sorrow had been turned into joy, and their mourning had been replaced with celebration. The transformation was so profound that the Jews established an annual feast, the feast of Purim, to commemorate their deliverance. Every year, they would remember how God had turned their sorrow into joy and how Esther's bravery had played a central role in their salvation.

Esther's choice to risk her life for her people was not just an act of personal bravery; it was an act that led to widespread transformation and deliverance. Her decision to stand up for what was right, even at great personal risk, resulted in the salvation of an entire nation. The story of Esther teaches us that one act of courage can have far-reaching effects, bringing about not only personal victory but also deliverance for others. Esther's bravery turned a time of great sorrow into a time of great joy, and her story continues to inspire people today to stand up for what is right, even when the odds seem insurmountable.

The feast of Purim, which was established to celebrate the Jews' deliverance, is a lasting reminder of the power of one person's choice to make a difference. It is a celebration of God's faithfulness, His protection, and His ability to turn even the darkest situations into moments of joy and victory. The Jews, who had once been mourning their impending destruction, were now rejoicing in their deliverance, and this joy was not just for a moment but became a part of their history and their identity as a people.

In conclusion, Esther's courageous choice resulted in monumental deliverance for her people, transforming a time of mourning into a time of joy. Her bravery in standing up for her people, even when it meant risking her own life, shows us the power of one person's actions to bring about widespread change. Esther's story is a powerful reminder that God can use anyone, no matter their background or circumstances, to accomplish His purposes. Through Esther's faith, wisdom, and courage, the Jewish people were saved from destruction, and their sorrow was turned into joy. Her story teaches us that when we act with courage and faith, trusting in God's plan, we can be part of something much larger than ourselves, something that brings about transformation and joy for others.

Conclusion

As we come to the conclusion of "For Such a Time: Esther's Courageous Stand", we are reminded that the lessons from Esther's life are not just stories from the past—they are a call to action for each of us today. Esther's journey of courage, faith, and sacrifice teaches us that God places us exactly where we need to be, even when the road ahead is uncertain or filled with fear. Just as Esther was called to step forward for her people "for such a time as this," we, too, are called to stand boldly in faith, even when the stakes are high. In a world full of challenges, injustice, and moments of deep uncertainty, the same God who gave Esther strength is with us now. We are called to rise, to be brave, and to trust that God is working through us for His greater purpose. The courage that Esther showed is the courage God asks of us—to stand for truth, justice, and love, no matter the cost. We may not always know the outcome, but we can be confident that God has a plan, and our faithfulness plays a role in it. As we face our own "for such a time as this" moments, may we remember that God is with us, empowering us to make a difference in the world, to shine His light, and to bring honor and glory to His name. Let Esther's courageous stand inspire you to trust in God's timing, to act with faith, and to believe that He is calling you to be courageous, just as He called Esther. Now, more than ever, we need to rise and stand boldly for God's truth and glory, for such a time as this.

Don't miss out!

Visit the website below and you can sign up to receive emails whenever Joshua Rhoades publishes a new book. There's no charge and no obligation.

https://books2read.com/r/B-A-AJLBB-RAGBF

BOOKS 2 READ

Connecting independent readers to independent writers.

Did you love *For Such a Time Esther's Courageous Stand*? Then you should read *The Immutable Fortress- Security in God's Unchanging Nature*[1] by Joshua Rhoades!

[2]

In a world that is constantly changing, where everything seems uncertain and unpredictable, the need for something solid and dependable is more important than ever. That's where God's unchanging nature comes in, like a fortress that cannot be shaken. The book, "The Immutable Fortress: Security in God's Unchanging Nature", invites readers to explore the comforting truth that, while everything around us may shift and change, God remains the same—yesterday, today, and forever. This book is about finding peace and security in knowing that God's character, promises, and love are unchangeable. When life gets hard, when we face challenges, or when we feel lost and unsure, we can find stability and hope in God's immutable nature. Just as a fortress provides protection and safety in the middle of a storm, God's unchanging nature offers us a safe place to stand, no matter what we are going through. Through stories, biblical truths, and practical applications, "The Immutable Fortress" shows us how to anchor our lives in God's unchanging character. It helps us understand that His promises are always trustworthy, His love is forever, and His power is constant. This book is a reminder that, no matter how much the world around us changes, we can always rely on God to be our rock and our refuge. In Him, we find the stability and security we need to face whatever comes our way, knowing that He is the same loving, just, and faithful God who has always been there for His people. So, if

---

1. https://books2read.com/u/3J21xK

2. https://books2read.com/u/3J21xK

you've ever felt overwhelmed by the changes and uncertainties of life, this book will guide you to the unshakable truth that God is your fortress, and in Him, you can find true and lasting security.